SCOOBY-DOO!
SPACE DISCOVERIES

EXPLORING PLANETS AND DWARF PLANETS WITH VELMA

by Ailynn Collins

CAPSTONE PRESS
a capstone imprint

Published by Capstone Press, an imprint of Capstone
1710 Roe Crest Drive
North Mankato, Minnesota 56003
capstonepub.com

Library of Congress Cataloging-in-Publication Data
is available on the Library of Congress website.
ISBN: 9781669021322 (hardcover)
ISBN: 9781669021179 (paperback)
ISBN: 9781669021285 (ebook PDF)

Summary: Science expert Velma and the rest of the Mystery Inc. gang are
ready to investigate planets and dwarf planets! Learn how the inner planets
are different from the outer planets, what the newest rovers are studying on
Mars, and more!

Editorial Credits
Editor: Carrie Sheely; Designer: Elyse White;
Media Researcher: Rebekah Hubstenberger;
Production Specialist: Whitney Schaefer

Image and Design Credits
Getty Images: adventtr, front cover (background), iStock/mdesigner125, 4-5
(background), Jamie Cooper, 5 (middle right), Meletios Verras, 22 (bottom),
Patrick T. Fallon/Bloomberg, 14 (bottom middle), Ron Miller/Stocktrek
Images, 23 (top), SCIEPRO/SCIENCE PHOTO LIBRARY, 21 (Uranus); NASA:
Ames/SETI Institute/JPL-Caltech, 28 (middle), ESA, 27 (bottom), Goddard
Space Flight Center, 17 (bottom), Johns Hopkins University Applied Physics
Laboratory/Southwest Research Institute, 24 (top right), JPL, 11 (Earth), JPL-
Caltech, 19 (bottom left), JPL-Caltech/MSSS, 15 (middle left), JPL-Caltech/
UCLA/MPS/DLR/IDA, 25 (top), JPL/MSSS, 12, JPL/Space Science Institute,
18 (top), JPL/USGS, 13 (bottom), JPL/Voyager 2, 21 (Neptune); Newscom:
Pictures From History, 29; Science Source: MARK GARLICK, 11 (top), Stuart
Painter, cover (bottom right), 1, 2-3, 30-31, 32; Shutterstock: cddesign.
co, design element (planets), Dima Zel, 13 (background), Grisha Bruev,
back cover (background), 6-7 (background), 10-11 (background), 14-15
(background), 21 (background), 24-25 (background), Grygorieva, 22-23
(background), helenpyzhova, 7 (top), KK.KICKIN, 8, 16-17 (background), 18-
19 (background), 26-27 (background), 28 (background), NASA images, 10
(middle), 11 (Venus), Vadim Sadovski, cover (top left)

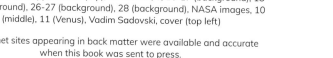

Printed and bound in China. PO5379

Table of Contents

Words in **bold** are in the glossary.

Our Solar System

The Mystery Inc. gang has arrived at their vacation spot. They relax around a campfire and gaze up at the nighttime sky.

Look! You can see Mars!

 Like, are there creepy aliens living there?

Ruh-roh! R-aliens?

 Not that we've found! But scientists are looking for signs that Mars had life long ago.

Mars is one of the eight planets in our **solar system**. Our solar system is made up of the sun, the planets, and all the rocks, dust, and gases in between. Everything is held in place by the sun's **gravity**.

Small space objects that orbit the sun are called dwarf planets or **asteroids**, depending on their size. These are mainly in the areas between planets.

Mars

FACT
The U.S. space agency, NASA, estimates that there are at least 100 billion planets in our Milky Way **Galaxy**. The Milky Way is a large group of stars that includes our solar system.

The word "planet" comes from the ancient Greek word for "wandering star." Most planets are named after characters from Greek myths.

Like, I'm going to wander into the house to see if I can find more marshmallows.

Me too!

People discovered the planets Mercury, Venus, Mars, Jupiter, and Saturn in ancient times. After **telescopes** were invented, scientists were able to see more planets. They discovered Uranus in 1781 and Neptune in 1846.

FACT
Astronomer William Herschel discovered Uranus by accident. He was doing a star survey when he saw it.

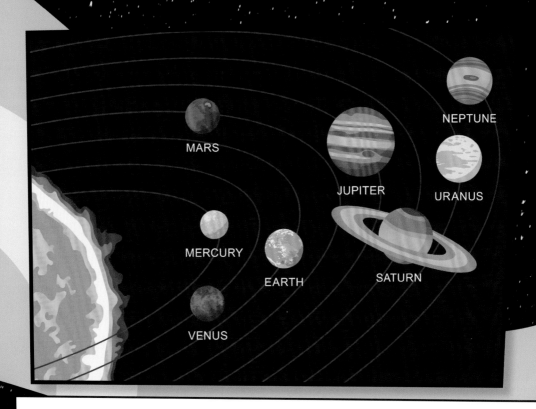

MARS

NEPTUNE

JUPITER

URANUS

MERCURY

EARTH

SATURN

VENUS

Over time, scientists came up with ways to categorize planets and other space objects. Today, a space object is called a planet if it has these three things:

- A planet must orbit a star, such as our sun.

- A planet must be round. Gravity pulls everything together in toward the middle. An object with strong enough gravity will eventually become round.

- A planet must be big enough so that its gravity has cleared away rocks and other space objects from its orbit around a star.

Chapter 1

The Inner Planets

The first four planets that are closest to the sun are known as the inner planets. They are Mercury, Venus, Earth, and Mars. These are rocky planets. They have hard surfaces made of metals and minerals called **silicates**.

The inner planets are close to one another. The outer planets are more spread out. Scientists measure distances between the planets and the sun in astronomical units (AU). One AU is the distance between Earth and the sun.

Planet Distances from Sun

Planet	Mercury	Venus	Earth	Mars	Jupiter	Saturn	Uranus	Neptune
Distance (AU)	0.39	0.72	1	1.52	5.2	9.54	19.2	30.06

Earth and some other planets have a layer of gas that surrounds them. This is called an atmosphere. Earth's atmosphere is made mostly of nitrogen and oxygen. These **elements** help make up the air we need to breathe. The atmosphere contains smaller amounts of other gases, such as carbon dioxide. The atmospheres of Venus and Mars are made almost completely of carbon dioxide. Humans wouldn't be able to breathe on either planet.

About 90 percent of Earth's crust is made of silicates. The soil we grow our food in is made up of a lot of silicates too! Scientists think they can help keep plants healthy.

Like, I'm all for anything that helps bring me more food! Right, Scoob?

Yeah!

Mercury is the planet closest to the sun. It has almost no atmosphere. Its gravity is too weak to hold onto the gases around it. Heat does not stay on the planet like it does on Earth. It can be as hot as 806 degrees Fahrenheit (430 degrees Celsius) in the daytime and as cold as -290°F (-180°C) at night.

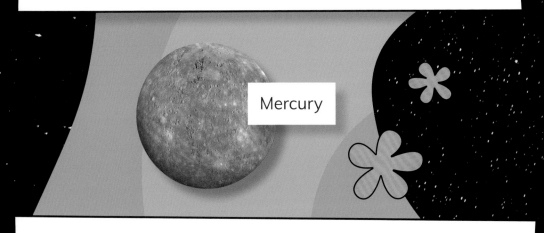

Mercury

Earth is the largest of the inner planets and the only one that has liquid water. Earth's atmosphere is perfect for protecting life on the planet. It keeps in the warmth from the sun. But it keeps out most of the sun's dangerous **radiation**.

Venus has a thick atmosphere. It forms a layer that traps heat inside, making the planet very hot all year. The temperature is about 900°F (480°C). It is the hottest planet in the solar system.

The thick atmosphere of Venus has clouds of sulfuric acid.

Scientists sometimes call Venus and Earth sister planets. They are nearly the same size. Scientists think they have a similar internal makeup too.

Earth

Venus

Mars is the fourth planet from the sun. The rust from the iron-filled materials on its surface makes Mars look red. That's why it's called the Red Planet.

Mars has craters and polar ice caps like Earth. But the ice on Mars is made of carbon dioxide. It's similar to the dry ice we use to keep things cold. The surface temperature of Mars is about -80°F (-60°C).

Scientists believe that there once was water on Mars. They think that the water **evaporated** into space a long time ago because the atmosphere of Mars is very thin. Since Mars might have had water, scientists believe Mars may have had life there.

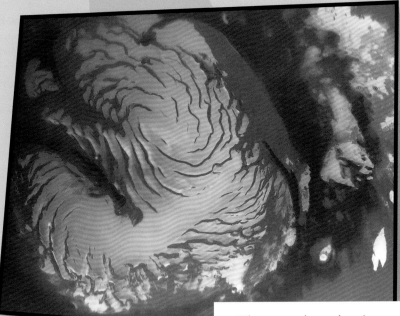

The north polar ice cap on Mars gets smaller in summer.

Some scientists think spacecraft would need to drill down deep to find signs that Mars once had life. On the surface, they think cosmic rays can destroy what living things need to survive.

Cosmic rays? Zoinks!

They enter Earth's atmosphere too. But Earth's atmosphere is thick. It provides protection.

That's a relief!

Mars' Huge Features

The largest volcano in the solar system is on Mars. It's called Olympus Mons. There's also a giant canyon called Valles Marineris. It's as long as the United States and takes up about one-fifth of Mars' surface.

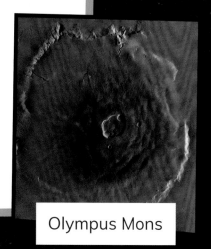

Olympus Mons

Space agencies from around the world have sent spacecraft to Mars. In 2018, NASA landed the InSight lander on Mars. It studied the planet's quake activity with a seisometer that sat on the surface. InSight picked up more than 1,000 quakes on Mars.

In 2012, NASA's Curiosity rover landed on Mars. It studies rocks and soil.

FACT

Diana Trujillo is a space engineer. She led the team that designed the robotic arm on Perseverance.

Diana Trujillo

Quakes on Mars are called "marsquakes." They're like earthquakes. They help scientists understand the planet's interior, such as the makeup and depth of the inner layers.

Maybe that's like when our stomachs rumble, Scoob! It says something about our interiors—they're empty!

Yeah, empty!

Perseverance travels over the rocky surface of Mars.

NASA's Perseverance rover landed on Mars in 2021. One of its jobs is to look for signs of life. Scientists chose a deep crater called the Jezero Crater for it to explore. This crater might have been a lake or river billions of years ago. Perseverance is collecting soil and rocks. Computers on board can find the tiniest proof of **organic material** in them.

Chapter 2

The Outer Planets

The outer planets are Jupiter, Saturn, Uranus, and Neptune. They're farther apart from one another than the inner planets. They're much bigger too.

Gases make up the atmosphere of these planets. They're mostly hydrogen and helium. There's no hard surface like the inner planets have. Scientists believe a liquid metal core is in the center of each gas giant.

The outer planets are also known as gas giants.

Speaking of gas giants, I know of another one!

Burp! Hee-hee!

Jupiter is the largest planet in the solar system. It has 300 times more **mass** than Earth.

Through telescopes on Earth, scientists can see a huge storm on Jupiter. Scientists have tracked it for about 150 years. They call it the Great Red Spot. It's wider than Earth, but it's getting smaller over time. Scientists don't know how or when it formed.

Scientists wonder if some of Jupiter's moons might be hiding liquid water under their frozen surfaces. If so, they may be able to support human life.

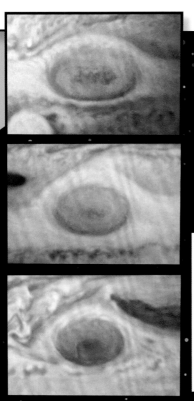

Jupiter

Comparison photos show how the Great Red Spot has been shrinking. The top photo is from 1995, the center one is from 2009, and the bottom photo is from 2014.

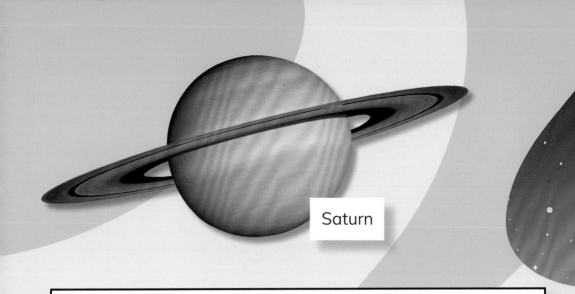

Saturn

Saturn has seven ring groups made of ice and rocks. There are four main groups and three narrower ones. These groups are made up of many smaller rings. All the outer planets have rings, but Saturn's are the most visible.

Saturn's main rings cover a large distance. They could reach almost from Earth to the moon! But the rings are very thin.

Cool! Imagine playing ring toss with rings that big!

From 2004 to 2017, the Cassini-Huygens spacecraft flew around Saturn 294 times. It took more than 450,000 photos. The photos helped scientists learn about the rocks and ice that make up the planet's rings.

Scientists are also interested in Saturn's moons. Cassini-Huygens found that the moon Enceladus had **geysers**. This means there could be hot water under the surface.

Scientists believe an ocean is deep underground on the moon Titan. NASA plans to launch a spacecraft called Dragonfly to land on Titan. Dragonfly's mission would be to search for signs of life.

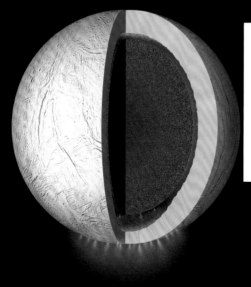

Scientists believe Enceladus has an icy crust, a global ocean, and a rocky core. The geysers erupt icy particles and water vapor from the moon's southern pole.

Uranus holds the record for the coldest temperature in our solar system—minus 371.56°F (minus 224.2°C).

Brrrrr! You couldn't dress in too many layers there! I'd use up my whole wardrobe and still be a popsicle!

I could lend you my scarf for a little splash of color!

Popsicle? Delicious!

Uranus and Neptune are sometimes called ice giants. They have icy, rocky cores. Uranus is the smallest of the outer planets in mass. But in size it's slightly larger than Neptune and four times wider than Earth.

The atmosphere of Uranus is made of gases including hydrogen, helium, and methane. The methane gas is what makes the planet look blue. Neptune's atmosphere mostly contains hydrogen. Like Uranus, it also has methane.

Uranus spins on its side. Some scientists think it may have been hit by a large asteroid, which caused it to fall. Others think it just tilted slowly over time. Uranus also spins in the opposite direction from most other planets.

Neptune

Uranus

Comparing the Gas Giants

Planet	Number of Moons	Number of Rings	Length of Day in Earth Hours	Time of One Orbit Around Sun
Jupiter	80-92	4	9 hours, 55 minutes	12 years
Saturn	83	7 groups	10 hours, 47 minutes	29 years
Uranus	27	13	17 hours, 14 minutes	84 years
Neptune	14	6	16 hours	165 years

Chapter 3

Dwarf Planets

In 2006, the International Astronomical Union (IAU) came up with the term "dwarf planet." Like a planet, a dwarf planet still must be round or nearly round. It must have enough gravity to hold all its parts together. It also must orbit a star. But a dwarf planet has not cleared out the area around its orbit.

The five recognized dwarf planets in our solar system are Pluto, Ceres, Eris, Haumea, and Makemake. They are in the asteroid belts. The main asteroid belt is between Mars and Jupiter. It's filled with rocks, asteroids, and other space objects.

Pluto   Eris   Haumea   Makemake   Ceres

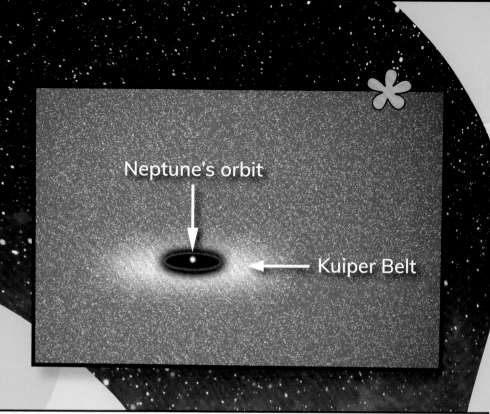

Neptune's orbit

Kuiper Belt

The asteroid belt beyond Neptune is the Kuiper Belt. It is a cold, dark place filled with millions of icy space objects. Some are small. Some are as big as 60 miles (100 km) across. This belt is home to most of the dwarf planets.

The Kuiper Belt is shaped like a doughnut!

Doughnut? Yum!

The first object the IAU called a dwarf planet was Pluto. It is the biggest known object in the Kuiper Belt. Many other planets have round orbital paths around the sun. But Pluto's is oval-shaped, or elliptical. Pluto spins on its side and takes six days to rotate once. Pluto has five moons.

Pluto

In 2006, Ceres was named a dwarf planet. It is the largest object in the main asteroid belt. Scientists believe it may have frozen water underground.

California astronomer Mike Brown and his team discovered Eris, Haumea, and Makemake. Eris is one of the largest dwarf planets in our solar system.

In 2015, the spacecraft Dawn went in orbit around Ceres. It was the first spacecraft to visit a dwarf planet. It found that bright areas in a crater on Ceres were mainly salt.

Like, cool! Now we know where to go if we ever need more salt, Scoob!

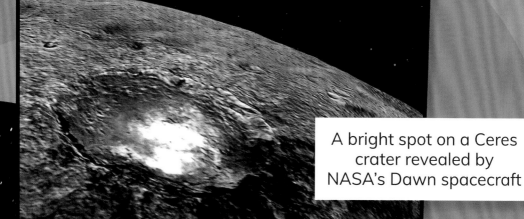

A bright spot on a Ceres crater revealed by NASA's Dawn spacecraft

Comparing Dwarf Planets

Name	Approximate Distance from Sun	Diameter	Time of One Orbit Around Sun	Year Discovered	Location
Ceres	257 million miles (m) (413 million km)	592 m (952 km)	4.6 years	1801	Main Asteroid Belt
Pluto	3.67 billion m (5.9 billion km)	1,430 m (2,302 km)	248 years	1930	Kuiper Belt
Eris	6.28 billion m (10.1 billion km)	1,445 m (2,326 km)	557 years	2003	Kuiper Belt
Haumea	4.01 billion m (6.4 billion km)	770 m (1,239 km)	285 years	2003	Kuiper Belt
Makemake	4.2 billion m (6.8 billion km)	888 m (1,429 km)	305 years	2005	Kuiper Belt

Chapter 4

Beyond our Solar System

So far, scientists have found more than 5,000 planets outside our solar system. These are called exoplanets.

Scientists discovered the first exoplanets in 1992. Space agencies want to learn more about these planets. They use space telescopes to help. Until its mission ended in 2018, the Kepler space telescope found more than 1,200 exoplanets. Today, NASA's Hubble Space Telescope helps scientists find exoplanets. Scientists also use ground telescopes to look into space.

In 2001, scientists found an exoplanet six times the mass of Jupiter. It was orbiting a star at about the same distance that Earth is from the sun. They called this area the habitable zone. Scientists think a planet orbiting at this distance may have life on it.

What kind of life?

It could be any kind, really. It could be tiny—so tiny it's microscopic!

Like, good news! Maybe it's something we can outrun, Scoob!

Yeah, phew!

Each exoplanet has unique features.

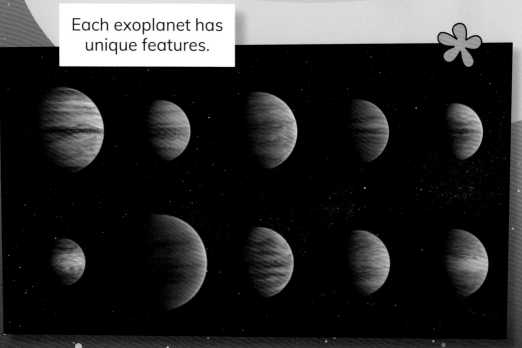

In 2014, the Kepler space telescope found an exoplanet a lot like Earth. Scientists named it Kepler-186f. It was about the same size as Earth, and it was in the habitable zone.

Scientists think Kepler-186f could be rocky like Earth.

In 2016, telescopes in Chili helped scientists discover Proxima b. It is the closest planet that is most like Earth.

In 2021, NASA launched the James Webb Space Telescope. It looks deeper into space than ever before. In September 2022, the James Webb telescope took the first direct image of an exoplanet. Who knows what else it will uncover in the future?

Extraordinary Engineer

Mary Golda Ross was a member of a top-secret project involved with designing advanced aircraft during World War II (1939-1945). A member of the Cherokee Nation, she was the only female engineer in the project. Ross also came up with designs for spaceships that might someday fly to distant planets. Her picture is on the 2019 Native American $1 coin. The coin was created to celebrate Native Americans in the space program.

Mary Golda Ross

Maybe someday, we'll have faster spaceships and we'll be able to see an exoplanet like Proxima b for ourselves.

For right now, I'm just happy to be here on our cozy home of Earth. I'll never take its air to breathe or its warmth for granted again!

Or its food!

Glossary

asteroid (AS-tuh-royd)—a large space rock that moves around the sun; asteroids are too small to be called planets

element (E-luh-muhnt)—a basic substance in chemistry that cannot be split into simpler substances

evaporate (i-VA-puh-rayt)—to change from a liquid into a vapor or a gas

galaxy (GAL-uhk-see)—a very large group of stars

geyser (GYE-zur)—an underground spring that shoots hot water and steam through a hole in the ground

gravity (GRAV-uh-tee)—a force that pulls objects together

mass (MASS)—the amount of physical matter an object contains

organic (or-GAN-ik)—related to living things

radiation (ray-dee-AY-shuhn)—tiny particles sent out from radioactive material

silicate (SI-luh-kayt)—a common mineral made of silicon and oxygen bound by metals such as iron, magnesium, and calcium

solar system (SOH-lurh SISS-tuhm)—system of planets and other bodies orbiting the sun; other planets around other stars are called planetary systems

telescope (TEL-uh-skope)—a tool people use to look at objects in space; telescopes make objects in space look closer than they really are

Read More

Dickmann, Nancy. *Exploring Space: Women Who Led the Way*. Scholastic: New York, 2022.

Labrecque, Ellen. *Earth and Other Planets*. North Mankato, MN: Capstone, 2020.

Ring, Susan. *Dwarf Planets*. AV2 Books: New York, 2020.

Internet Sites

DK Findout!: The Solar System
dkfindout.com/us/space/solar-system/

Kiddle: Planet Facts for Kids
kids.kiddle.co/Planet

NASA Space Place
spaceplace.nasa.gov/menu/solar-system/

Index

About the Author

Ailynn Collins has written many books for children. Science and space are among her favorite subjects. She has an MFA in writing for Children and Young Adults from Hamline University and has spent many years as a teacher. She lives outside Seattle with her family and five dogs.